Talking to My Mum

Talking to My Mum

A Picture Workbook for Workers, Mothers and Children Affected by Domestic Abuse

Cathy Humphreys, Ravi K. Thiara, Agnes Skamballis and Audrey Mullender

Foreword by June Freeman
Illustrations by Suzan Aral

Jessica Kingsley Publishers
London and Philadelphia

First published in 2006
by Jessica Kingsley Publishers
116 Pentonville Road
London N1 9JB, UK
and
400 Market Street, Suite 400
Philadelphia, PA 19106, USA

www.jkp.com

Copyright © Cathy Humphreys, Ravi K. Thiara, Agnes Skamballis, Audrey Mullender and
Colchester and Tendring Women's Refuge 2006
Foreword copyright © June Freeman 2006
Illustrations copyright © Suzan Aral 2006
Illustration on page 84 copyright © Beate Alldis 2006

The right of Cathy Humphreys, Ravi K. Thiara, Agnes Skamballis and Audrey Mullender to be
identified as authors of this work has been asserted by them in accordance with the Copyright,
Designs and Patents Act 1988.

British Library Cataloguing in Publication Data
A CIP catalogue record for this book is available from the British Library

ISBN 978 1 84310 422 3

Printed and bound in Great Britain by
MPG Books Limited, Cornwall

Contents

Acknowledgements

Our first acknowledgement goes to Colchester and Tendring Women's Refuge (CTWR) for their role in securing Big Lottery Funding for this project and their ongoing collaboration and inspiration in the research.

In addition, however, many other people have contributed in important ways to this resource. We would like to thank:

- the mothers and children who worked on the activities and helped us develop the ideas for this resource

- workers from the seven refuges which comprise Refuge Essex, as well as those from Milton Keynes, Panahghar and York; counsellors and support workers with the NSPCC in York and Cheshire; the Domestic Violence Intervention Project in London and the Rape Crisis Centre in Colchester

- all managers in refuges and the NSPCC who supported the work

- Suzan Aral and Beate Alldis for the graphics and the work on the design of the original workbook

- Donna Packham and others who helped with reworking the activities

- the Advisory Group run by Colchester and Tendring Women's Refuge, who have worked with us throughout the project, offered us ideas and debated with us

- Stephen Jones and Leonie Sloman from Jessica Kingsley Publishers for their help with publication.

We have also adapted activities which have been developed and used elsewhere. In particular, Barnardos Northern Ireland has a wonderful pack for children from which we have drawn some ideas. Other activities like the Tree of Life (The Feelings Tree) and the protective behaviours 'hand' have been in use since the 1980s and have been adapted to be used with mothers and children in this resource.

For further information, please contact:
Talking to My Mum
c/o Colchester and Tendring Women's Refuge
PO Box 40
Colchester
Essex CO1 2XJ, UK
info@colchester-refuge.org.uk
www.colchester-refuge.org.uk

Foreword

This resource was born out of the growing concern for abused women and children living in refuges. Historically refuges were set up to help women who wanted to escape their partners' violence. From the beginning, however, women brought their children with them and refuges took them in.

As a result refuges soon found they were accommodating, on average, twice as many children as women. Something had to be done, if only to cope with the management of the noise and turbulence children always generate. But refuge staff also began to notice children who were unnaturally quiet, children who threatened to burst with aggression, children who glued themselves to their mothers and whose screams threatened to bring the house down if she left the room without them. There were also the 10-and 12-year-olds who wet their beds and the children who suffered from terrible nightmares. As refuge workers learnt more about the mothers' experiences, however, their real surprise was that so many refuge children were so normal. Yet, while their admiration for the resilience of children who'd lived with domestic violence grew, so did the evidence that such children badly needed understanding, care and attention in their own right.

For years, however, refuges had to muddle along, getting people to give a few hours a week to run play groups, though it was obvious that play sessions scarcely scratched the surface of what was needed. Children who had lived with domestic violence had special needs and required specially trained staff.

When the Big Lottery Fund launched a research programme, Colchester and Tendring Women's Refuge was therefore immediately interested. Like many other refuges we had replaced the title of playworker with the more appropriate title of childworker some time ago, but still only had two part-time children's staff. Undeterred we made contact with the University of Warwick where much of the cutting edge academic work on children living with domestic violence was being done. A year, and a lot of hard work, later we had a partnership with Warwick, a grant and a research team.

The first aim of the research has been to construct a practical programme of action, for helping children who have lived with domestic violence. This programme has adopted a perspective which has received too little official attention to date, namely, the need to facilitate quality communication between such children and their mothers.

Following some sensational cases of child abuse and subsequent public concern about child protection, current thinking has emphasised the child's rights as an individual and tended to concentrate on the need to keep children out of danger. Despite the good intentions behind this as a policy it can be deeply alienating socially for the child. It also diverts attention from the fact that human beings develop into secure and socially productive adults through positive and constructive interaction with significant others. Hence the title of the overall research project: Talking to My Mum. It is vital for the social growth of abused mothers and their children that they find ways of working through the experience of living with domestic violence together.

The research method adopted was that of action research. This deliberately blurred the divide between researchers and participants and it ensured that the responses of mothers and their children trying to deal with living with domestic violence would continually shape the course of the project. It also constantly alerted the researchers to the conditions needed for constructive and healing conversations to take place between abused women and their children.

Even routine interaction with children is high octane work and it was increasingly clear that women, ground down by abusive relationships, needed to regain some personal equilibrium before they could explore the issues their children had. The idea of 'readiness' that the researchers discuss in the manual was found to be critically important.

The research project on which this book is based has been a positive and fruitful exercise. First and foremost, it has developed a practical programme for helping abused women and their children forge a relationship that could help them move towards fully realising their capacities as productive members of society. Subsequent academic publications will develop more generally the ideas that shaped this programme. The project has shown that small front line organisations and large academic institutions can work positively and fruitfully together when they are joined by good will and passionately committed to the same social goal.

June Freeman
Colchester and Tendring Women's Refuge
Chair of the Steering Committee

Introduction and guidance

The activities in this workbook have been developed with the help of mothers and children who have lived with domestic abuse. Workers from refuges, outreach services and community-based programmes working with women and young people have also guided us in thinking about activities that were helpful and about what was needed. While we take responsibility for the final book, we want to emphasise that this has been a joint effort, to which at least 100 people have contributed.

This resource is part of an action research project that involved working with mothers and children to understand better the effects of domestic abuse on their relationships with each other. At the same time, activities were created with the help of mothers, workers and children to develop and build on the communication between them so that they were not waiting until the end of the project to find out what might be helpful, but instead the ideas were put into action as we went along.

Comments from mothers

It's definitely helped talking about issues that worry myself or him. And I've also learnt to explain things to him, difficult issues, rather than push it to one side. (Sandra, mother of two children)

It felt like through talking to each other we could lighten our hearts. The children were interested in what we were doing and through this they asked a lot of questions about what happened. It was a really good opportunity for me to feel my children's sadness and happiness. (Manreet, mother of three children)

Comments from children

It was fun, and a good way of spending time with Mum instead of just doing my own thing, watching TV or playing on my PlayStation. It was something different and it was spending time with my mum. (Raj, 11-year-old boy)

It was fun, I got to spend time with Mum and talk about what happened. It made me think about the things that had happened. (Sarah, ten-year-old girl)

Who is this workbook for?

The activities were developed for mothers and children who have lived with domestic abuse. This resource was particularly developed for younger children. Another workbook, *Talking about Domestic Abuse*, is available for older children, young people and their mothers.

The material is tailored for use by a wide range of professionals working with families which have experienced domestic abuse, including refuge workers, children's workers, counsellors, psychologists, family therapists, health visitors and social workers. It is also suitable for mothers to use independently with their children or with guidance from a professional. If you are using the material independently as a mother who has experienced domestic abuse, we offer advice on when and where it is appropriate to use the material. For the most part we have found that children under five find a lot of the activities unsuitable. However, the upper age limit depends very much on the child. There are many activities in common between this resource and *Talking about Domestic Abuse*, but the way in which the material is presented in the latter differs, to appeal to older children.

Mothers and children from different ethnic backgrounds who helped develop the activities found that sometimes they needed more help from workers when English was not their first language. This can also be true for mothers and children for whom reading does not come easily, so you will notice that these activities have a strong visual element.

Most of the activities are about having 'quality time' together, helping to build the young person's self-esteem, learning to talk about feelings and developing communication and understanding between mothers and their children. Therefore, while *Talking to My Mum* has primarily been written for mothers and children who have experienced domestic abuse, it may also be helpful for all mothers and children, not just those who have been through domestic abuse. Some mothers may be unsure whether they have been living with domestic abuse or not. When there has not been any physical violence, or very limited use of physical force, then it can be particularly confusing for mothers and children to know whether they have suffered domestic abuse.

If women are still living with domestic abuse, then some of the activities may not be appropriate. There may not be a safe enough place to talk about some of the issues that are raised, which may put the mother or child in a difficult position. Even the subtitle of this resource may create danger, as perpetrators of domestic abuse do not usually like the issue to be named so clearly in this way.

This brings us to the question of dads. Many workers have suggested that fathers (whether they were abusers or not) are also in need of a resource such as this. While we agree, we have not consulted with fathers about the development of these activities. That would be an important but different project.

Another issue that is important to bear in mind when using this material is whether the person is ready. Are the mother and her child in a position to be able to concentrate and spend 10 to 15 minutes of quality time together at least twice a week? It may not sound a lot, but if a mother is newly separated and dealing with new housing, new schools, managing health problems or having difficulty sleeping, she may not feel that it is the right moment to be doing these activities.

A woman using these materials with her child also needs to be in a place where she is not so worried about her own survival that she is unable to hear and listen to what is happening to the child. Some aspects of the workbook require a readiness to see and hear that the child has been affected by the domestic abuse as well, and this can be painful.

However, many of the activities in the workbook are just about relaxing and having some fun together. Again, if you are feeling low it may be difficult to find the energy to spend this time with your child. So not all mothers will be ready to do this. Mothers need to be in a position where this time to be with their child or children is possible.

Do mothers need a support person?

The activities have all been developed and tried out with women and children as 'stand-alone' activities where they do not need a worker to be with them to do the activities. However, we would recommend that mothers have someone they can 'check in' with on a regular basis so that support is available when it is needed.

Most women tell us that at points along the way they have really appreciated the support of someone, usually a refuge worker or a counsellor, particularly when children let them know how much they have remembered, seen or heard. If a woman has worked hard to be protective of her child or children, then understanding how they have been affected by domestic abuse can be upsetting. At other times it can be reassuring to know how well they are getting along.

Women and children also tell us that it is easier to find the motivation and time to keep doing the activities together if there is someone to talk to who is interested in following up what they are doing. A support person can provide this added source of encouragement.

Many workers find that 'take-home' activities help when they are working with mothers or children and that these are a way of strengthening and encouraging the changes being made in individual or group sessions.

What do we know about domestic abuse?

If women have lived with domestic abuse, then they are the experts on what this means for them. However, they have told us that they find it helpful to have a 'bigger picture' because the nature of domestic abuse can make it hard to see it for what it is. At the heart of domestic abuse there is usually someone who wants to blame the victim for the abuse they are experiencing – that somehow it is all their fault. This 'messed up' thinking can make women and children feel as though they are 'going crazy' and it can make it hard to name domestic abuse.

Here are two frequently asked questions about domestic abuse.

What is domestic abuse?

Domestic abuse or domestic violence typically involves physical, sexual and emotional abuse and intimidation, which often escalates in frequency and severity over time. Emotional abuse can include intimidation, harassment, damage to property, threats and financial abuse. It can be understood as the misuse of power and exercise of control by one partner over the other in an intimate relationship. Children living with domestic abuse can also suffer harm either from the same person who is hurting their mother or by hearing or seeing the harm which their mother is experiencing.

Domestic abuse and domestic violence are the same thing. Women often prefer the term domestic abuse because it seems to describe more clearly the emotional and mental abuse which can be more frequent than physical abuse. Sometimes actual physical abuse does not occur. Other people prefer the term domestic violence because it recognises the seriousness of the abuse as violence (even if this is emotional violence) and helps to acknowledge that much of the violence is a crime and should be treated as a crime.

Is a man always the abuser and how many people are affected?

More women than men report being the victims of domestic abuse. The British Crime Survey showed that 13 per cent of women and 9 per cent of men reported some form of domestic abuse.[1] However, when the most serious abuse is considered, based on the number of attacks, the range of forms of violence and the severity of injury, women are overwhelmingly the most victimised. Women are twice as likely to be injured, and three times as likely to report living in fear than men: 90 per cent of incidents of domestic abuse reported to the police involved a female victim and a male perpetrator.[2]

Some women also report that the man's relatives, including mothers and sisters, can be involved in the abuse. Men and women in same-sex relationships report the same levels of domestic abuse as those in heterosexual relationships. Disabled women report that their carers, sometimes but not always including their partners, can be involved in domestic abuse.

1 Walby, S. and Allen, J. (2004) *Domestic Violence, Sexual Assault and Stalking: Findings from the British Crime Survey.* Home Office Research Study 276. London: Home Office Research, Development and Statistics Directorate.
2 Scottish Executive 2003.

A UK study of 2869 young adults showed that 26 per cent had witnessed violence between their parents at least once and for 5 per cent the violence was frequent and ongoing.[3] Each year 23,500 children will live in a refuge, escaping from the violence with their mothers.[4] The Department of Health estimates that 750,000 children in the UK are living with domestic abuse.[5] In other words, domestic abuse is a widespread social problem. It has been estimated to cost employers £1.3 billion a year and the government £3.1 billion a year in the UK alone. This includes the costs through the criminal justice system, health care, social services, housing and civil legal services.[6] It does not include the human and emotional costs, which are huge.

An attack on the mother–child relationship

The reason that this resource for mothers and children has been developed is because research undertaken by ourselves and others shows that domestic abuse also needs to be understood as an attack on the relationship between mothers and their children.[7] This may be the direct undermining of the relationship between mothers and children through mothers being criticised and insulted in front of their children, or where children are encouraged to be physically and verbally abusive towards their mothers. It may be more indirect through mothers needing to make sure that their partner's needs come first all the time, or mothers becoming depressed and anxious and therefore having difficulty parenting. Sometimes women may be physically hurt by an attack and unable to act as a parent for a time. Children may become very close to their mothers, but may need to deal with the 'adult world' in helping to support them through a difficult time. There are many, many ways in which hurting the relationship between mothers and their children can be part of the abuse.

Only a small proportion of mothers and their children may actually be able to talk together about the domestic abuse. It can be like 'the elephant in the living room' – obvious to everybody but everyone also pretending that it is not there.

Whatever their situation, mothers and children experience a period of transition and change when they separate from a situation of domestic abuse.

3   Gorin, S. (2004) *Understanding What Children Say: Children's Experiences of Domestic Violence, Parental Substance Misuse and Parental Health Problems.* London: National Children's Bureau and NSPCC.
4   www.womensaid.org.uk
5   Department of Health (2003) *Women's Mental Health: Into the Mainstream.* London: The Stationery Office.
6   Walby, S. (2004) *The Cost of Domestic Violence.* London: Women and Equality Unit.
7   Mullender, A., Kelly, L., Hague, G., Malos, E. and Iman, U. (2002) *Children's Perspectives on Domestic Violence.* London: Routledge.

Sometimes children don't know how to react when they are no longer living with the same level of fear. Sometimes women don't know how to react when they have to 'get into the driver's seat' because in the past they have been allowed to make very few decisions. There are many changes to get used to.

We have developed these activities because we have heard from mothers, children and workers that leaving a situation of domestic abuse does not immediately make everything better. Everyone needs time to recover and to work out how to live in a different situation. Being able to communicate how mothers and children are feeling and how they experience their situation can help this process along. This is what we hope these activities will help mothers and children to do.

What is in the workbook?

The workbook is made up of different activities for mothers and children to do together. It is a good idea to start with the introductory activity and then introduce the woodland animals. Each animal has a different idea or theme which links it to different activities. There is sometimes an activity with the animals followed by a similar activity for mothers and children.

The workbook is divided into three sections:

1. Early days – activities for getting started and activities to address any recent changes in living arrangements.

2. Talking about things that matter – activities for opening up talking points – about both the present and the past.

3. Moving on – activities for leaving, finishing a group or moving to a new place.

Each activity has a set of traffic lights to signal 'stop', 'getting worried' or 'keep going'. Not all mothers and children use these, but some children use them a lot to let their mothers know how they are doing with an activity without having to say anything.

Should mothers and children do every activity?

Not necessarily! We recommend a 'pick and mix approach' where mothers and children (and often a worker) choose a range of different activities which they would like to do together, and which seems most appropriate to them.

Activities have been developed to reflect the different experiences of mothers and children – what is right for one child and their mother isn't necessarily right for another. Every activity in this workbook has been tested with women and children and was found to be really helpful or positive for at least some people. Mothers and children don't need to do them all to experience lots of benefits.

What if a woman has more than one child?

Whether to use these materials with one child or with all the children is up to the family. In testing these activities, mothers had very different approaches to this issue. One child might really want to do the activities and another not at all. One child might be in need of some 'quality time' and special attention. The resource provides activities which allow mothers to give this time. Other mothers have tried doing activities with all of their children – or at least setting up something for one child to do while sitting down with another. Sometimes a friend or worker can help out if a mother needs quality time with just one child, or if a child is too young or too old to be involved.

Can mothers and children write or draw in the pack?

The activity sheets for mothers and children are fully photocopiable, but equally a family can write and draw in it together if they have their own workbook.

Sometimes writing or drawing might feel like 'hard work'. The activities are to help mothers and children talk and play together. They can be used to help mothers and children talk together if they don't feel like writing down answers to questions.

The advantage of writing and drawing is that there is a record that mothers and children can both look back on together or something which can be easily shared with a worker.

Mothers and children who helped to develop these activities found that drawing and talking are often more fun than writing. Although a space may look as though it is created for writing, drawing and talking can work just as well or better – do what works for you. Women who have difficulty reading in English may need support from a worker or friend.

Introduction for mothers

Before getting started, it may be helpful to sit down with a support person and go through some things together. Some of the points below may be helpful reminders before starting:

- First, and most importantly, the way women think about themselves is often one of the more damaging after-effects of the abuse they have suffered. Rebuilding yourself as a person, looking after yourself and learning to think about yourself as positive and worthwhile are as important as helping your children to think about themselves in a positive way. Children's recovery is often linked to their mother's recovery from abuse experiences.

- Children look to the most important people in their social network to build their sense of self. One of the most important people (often *the* most important person) is the child's mother. This is why we have developed activities for you to do with your child.

- Mothers often try extremely hard to stop their children from being hurt by the violence and abuse which they are experiencing. It is not their fault that they have been hurt and experienced domestic abuse. Nor is it their fault that this may have affected aspects of their relationship with their children. It may be worth remembering some of the ways in which you have tried to protect your child and share these with a worker or support person, or just write them down as a reminder for yourself.

Things I did to try to protect my child or children

1. . . . .
. . . .
. . . .

2. . . . .
. . . .
. . . .

3. . . . .
. . . .
. . . .

What are some of the positive things in the relationship with your child which you will be building on when you are working together on these activities?

1. . . . .
. . . .
. . . .

2. . . . .
. . . .
. . . .

3. . . . .
. . . .
. . . .

Ground rules for getting started

1.   There are no right or wrong answers, correct or incorrect ways of doing the activity sheets.

2.   Sometimes your child may be very distracted and not want to play with the activity sheets. Don't force the issue, just try again some other time. It may be that it is not the right activity for them so perhaps try something else.

3.   For younger children we have a traffic light code on the activity sheets – with 'stop', 'getting worried' and 'keep going' – which may be helpful.

4.   Some children are very active and will need to be engaged in more physical activities. A list of suggestions is provided at the back of the workbook.

5.   Choosing the right time can be really important. You will have to plan when is the right time for you. You may need a children's worker or friend to look after your other children while you do this. Ten or 15 minutes of quality time may be all that is needed for each activity.

6.   Privacy is important. This is your child's time with you. You will need to talk about whether you can share with other people what you have done together. Sometimes your child will want to share, sometimes they may wish to remain private. We know this can be difficult if you live with other people, particularly in a refuge.

7.   Sometimes your child may tell you things that distress you and are hard for you to hear. These occasions may not be easy for you. However, this is a moment of trust and it is important to try to listen and to respond to what your child is saying to you. It is also a time when you may need to see a worker for some extra support. Five positive responses to your child are:

     • I believe you.

     • I am glad you told me this.

     • I am sorry that this happened to you.

     • It is not your fault and never was.

     • I am here for you and if you want to talk more about this you can.

This workbook is important for children. Finding the words and trying to understand your child (even when they are being difficult) is a challenge for every mother and may be even harder when you have come through a tough time together. There is much to celebrate as well as many barriers to get over.

Tips for workers

Many people who work with women and children affected by domestic abuse have contributed to this workbook. In their experience, the services for women and children have become separated in ways that are inappropriate and unhelpful, and this book provides ways of bridging this divide. We recognise that the best resource for children is to have a mother who is in a position to be able to love, protect and understand them and that anything which workers can do to strengthen and support this relationship is extremely positive. A number of ideas for workers using this workbook have emerged from their experiences:

- Act as a support person for mothers and children, check in with them regularly and actively encourage them in working on the activities together. In particular, it is good to be there at times when difficult issues arise. Women often need emotional back-up to continue if activities bring to the surface strong feelings and memories raised by their children.

- Use the activities as 'take-home' activities to support other group or individual work you are already doing with mothers and/or their children.

- Children's workers should have the workbooks visible and easily accessible so that children can become interested and excited by the activities they are shown, and the inclusion of mothers becomes a natural extension of this work.

- Advocates and support workers for women should have the workbooks in view or in the waiting room, which can provide an easy means for women to access the resource. Most women are very keen to strengthen the relationships with their children. However, be aware of the issue of 'readiness'. These activities work best for women and children who are not in a chaotic or crisis situation.

- Look after other children in the family if it has been agreed that the mother spend 'special time' with one child either due to the difficulties they are experiencing or due to age or time constraints for the other children.

- Photocopy the activities so that they can be used by many women and young people as they pass through the service.

- A reflection sheet and feedback form has been placed towards the back of the workbook. If mothers and children want to let workers know how they felt about an activity, it is useful to photocopy this sheet for them to fill in.

Final comments from mothers

You've got to learn to talk to your children. They are young people but they fully understand. And you've got to explain to them what is going on. And that's what I've learnt with him. (Jenny, mother of an eight-year-old boy)

To talk, rather than to argue, we've learnt not to war... And for me to stay calm as well in a situation. (Deidre, mother of two children)

Final comments from children

I wanted to do it because it would help me to understand my mum's feelings and my feelings. And it did help. I could let out my feelings and tell her what's locked up in my heart. (Kirah, ten years)

It would be good for other children and their mums. If they went through what my mum went through, it could help them to understand each other and what happened. (Aisha, ten years)

Further information

Helpful phone numbers and websites for women and young people in the UK, USA, Australia and Canada are listed at the back of this workbook.

SECTION I

EARLY DAYS

Activity 1: Me and my mum

This activity is to get you started and used to the idea of spending some time together on the *Talking to My Mum* activities.

This activity helps you to focus on the positive things about each other.

Naming people can help you to identify and talk about important people in your child's life. However, this may also raise issues about people who you may not be in touch with at the moment or who have been hurtful to either you or your child. There is no easy way to deal with this. It is just important that you listen and help them identify people they think are important. It may also raise happy memories about people who care about you and your child.

The Magic Mirror is a fun way of helping children to say something about who they are. A good way for this to be a shared activity and for you to reinforce your child's sense of self is to take things that you know your child likes and make the frame as suggested.

If your child is reluctant to draw, you may like to use a photograph instead. The important thing is for you both to do the activity together.

At the end you may want to put the magic mirror on your fridge or stick it somewhere where it can be seen.

After you finish you may like to ask each other what it was like to do this activity together.

Me and my mum

Me about my mum:

You would know my mum because she has:

. . . . eyes and . . . . hair.

She is . . . . tall. She is . . . . years old.

Her name is . . . .

My mum is special because . . . .

. . . .

My mum about me:

You would know my child because she/he has:

. . . . eyes and . . . . hair.

She/he is is . . . . years and . . . . months old.

Her/his name is . . . .

She/he is special because: . . . .

. . . .

Important people in her/his life are: . . . .

. . . .

Magic mirror

When I look in the magic mirror this is what I see:

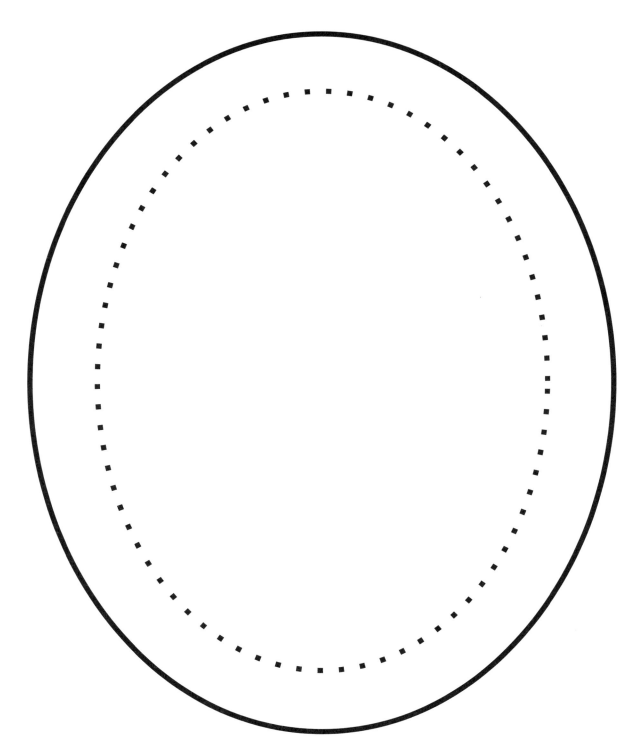

You could also ask your mum to write or draw things around the mirror which remind her of you. For example, she might like to decorate it with flowers or hearts or diamonds or shells or stars or footballs or cars or words that describe you.

Activity 2: Your new friends

We have used different woodland animals to represent different themes. Sometimes it is easier to use animals to talk about feelings which may be hard to express. Your child may like to spend time colouring in the different friends while you introduce each animal.

The traffic lights are used so that your child can let you know how they are feeling as they do each activity with you. You may like to use the traffic lights to check in with them from time to time.

Your new friends

Here are some friends who want to join in the activities (you may want to colour them in to brighten them up).

TAZ the tortoise
who likes to sit around and has lots of great ideas about keeping safe

OLLIE the owl
who is always on the lookout for new information

JAS the butterfly and CAS the caterpillar
who look different but are related

BAS the bear
who has learned to live with big changes

PRICKLES the hedgehog and NIBBLES the squirrel who like to listen to how people are feeling

Who is your favourite?

There are also TRAFFIC LIGHTS like these on each page which you can use together to point out when you want to STOP, when you are GETTING WORRIED or when you want to KEEP GOING.

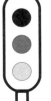

STOP

GETTING WORRIED

KEEP GOING

Activity 3: Exploring the place where you live

This is a 'doing' activity so that you and your child can spend some active time together. You may even think of some more questions as you explore the place where you live.

For some children who have recently moved to a new place this allows safe exploration and helps them to feel more at home in their new surroundings.

Activity 4 is written for children and their mothers who have moved to a refuge or hostel. Skip Activity 3 and move to Activity 4 if you live in a hostel or refuge.

OLLIE's quiz: exploring the place where you live

OLLIE is in a new place. She is having to go around and find out lots of things. Can you and your mum help **OLLIE** answer her questions? You may be able to do this by just sitting still or you might need to go and explore.

- How many rooms are there in the place where you live? . . . .

- How many people stay in your house? . . . .

- Is there an outdoor play area? . . . .

- How many windows are there in the place where you live? . . . .

- Do you know the names of any other children who live nearby? What are they?

  . . . .

- What colour is the kitchen? . . . .

- Can you count the number of stairs in the place where you live? . . . .

Do you or OLLIE have any other questions about the place where you live that you want the answers to?

. . . .

. . . .

. . . .

. . . .

. . . .

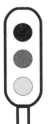

STOP

GETTING WORRIED

KEEP GOING

. . . .

. . . .

. . . .

Activity 4: Exploring the refuge

This activity is for mothers and children living in a refuge.

Moving to a refuge can be a very big change for children. Some children will find the change a relief and will enjoy mixing with other children. However, it can also be frightening if you do not know the place where you live and that you share with lots of other people. Helping your child to be curious and actively explore their surroundings can be fun and help them to feel more at ease.

This activity may raise some issues for your child and you about the place where you used to live. If this happens you may want to spend some time talking about this.

OLLIE's quiz: exploring the refuge

When you first come to the refuge it can feel very different from where you have lived before.

OLLIE is in a new place. She is having to go around and find out lots of things. Can you and your mum help **OLLIE** answer her questions? You may be able to do this by just sitting still or you might need to go and explore and ask other people (including workers) some questions.

- How many rooms are there for families in this refuge? . . . .

- How many people can sleep in your family's room? . . . .

- What time is the playroom open for children your age? . . . .

- Is there an outdoor play area? . . . .

- What is the name of the children's worker or any worker you have played with?

  . . . .

- Do you know the names of any other children living in the refuge? What are they?

  . . . .

- What colour is the kitchen? . . . .

- If families eat in a shared area, how many tables are there? . . . .

- Are children allowed in the cooking area? . . . .

- Can you count the number of stairs inside the refuge? . . . .

STOP

GETTING WORRIED

KEEP GOING

Do you or OLLIE have any other questions about the refuge you want the answers to?

. . . .

. . . .

Activity 5: Changes I like and things I miss

Change usually brings many positive benefits but it also raises difficult issues. This is true for both adults and children. Some children may feel very confused when there are major changes in their lives. This activity is designed for you to explore with them both the negative and the positive aspects of the changes in your lives and to help them understand that while something can be good there can also be some painful feelings. Not all children will have this experience but don't be surprised if your child does.

In doing this activity, it is important for you to support your child in understanding that it is possible and acceptable to have both kinds of feeling. For those children who can only think of things that they miss, you will need to help them find one or two positive changes that you have noticed. You may like to share one or two things that have been positive for you, however small.

Changes I like and things I miss

BAS the cuddly bear has lived in many different places. His last home was a forest but he has learnt to be happy in his new life as a teddy bear tucked up in a bed, or with his friends in the playroom. There are things he misses and changes he likes.

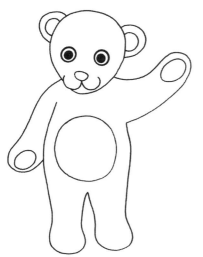

Things BAS misses	Changes BAS likes
trees	*warm beds*
wild honey	*honey from the fridge*
forest friends	*new friends*
forest noises	*feeling safe*

You and Mum will also have things in your life that you miss as well as changes that you like. What are they?

Things I miss	Changes I like
. . . .	. . . .
. . . .	. . . .
. . . .	. . . .
. . . .	. . . .
. . . .	. . . .
. . . .	. . . .
. . . .	. . . .

STOP

GETTING WORRIED

KEEP GOING

Activity 6: Match the feelings

Children often find it hard to know what they are feeling. It is an important skill to learn to name feelings and it is one of the most important things that mothers can help their children with. If children can't say what they are feeling, this will affect their behaviour. Some children may act out aggressively, others may withdraw. Either situation can be painful.

This activity helps you to use the animals' feelings to begin to identify feelings, which may also apply to your child. To help you to do this, you may want to ask your child what might make Prickles and Nibbles feel happy, sad, excited, scared, etc. A further step might be to ask your child what makes them feel happy, sad, scared, excited, etc.

Help NIBBLES the squirrel and PRICKLES the hedgehog to match the feeling

Sometimes it is hard to know what you are feeling, especially if you are having a tough time. Sometimes you just want to run away. Other times you feel like crying. But sometimes you just feel like laughing.

NIBBLES and **PRICKLES** are showing different feelings. Can you draw a line to match the feeling to the animal? Can you imagine what might make **NIBBLES** and **PRICKLES** feel this way? Ask Mum to help you draw the lines.

Happy

Sad

Scared

Hurt and upset

Excited

Angry

STOP

GETTING WORRIED

KEEP GOING

Activity 7: The same and different

This activity is a fun way of finding out more about each other and recognising that everyone doesn't have to be the same. Having things in common is enjoyable but it is just as important to appreciate each other's differences. For children it is particularly important for their development to separate themselves in small but positive ways from their parents. Children often enjoy finding out a little more about their mothers. You may not have had the chance to share this kind of information with each other in the past.

The same and different

JAS the butterfly and **CAS** the caterpillar are related (Mum might need to explain how if you don't know). They are different but sometimes they like the same things.

Ways they are alike

Both like plants and flowers

Both like sunny days

Both need to hide from birds

Both live in the garden

Ways they are different

Butterflies have wings

Caterpillars can't fly

Caterpillars eat more

Caterpillars have more legs

My favourite things

You and your mum will have things you both like and other things that are different.

Favourite music

Me . . . . Mum . . . .

Favourite colour

Me . . . . Mum . . . .

Favourite TV programme

Me . . . . Mum . . . .

Favourite food

Me . . . . Mum . . . .

Favourite drink

Me . . . . Mum . . . .

Favourite thing to do

Me . . . . Mum . . . .

Favourite person outside the family

Me . . . .

Mum . . . .

STOP

GETTING WORRIED

KEEP GOING

Activity 8: About safety

Safety is one of the biggest issues for mothers and children who have lived with domestic abuse. A sense of both emotional and physical safety is important for children's development. Physical safety can be created through establishing clear rules and expectations. This can be a difficult activity as children are often more aware of what makes them scared than what makes them feel safe. You will probably need to help them with thinking about 'staying safe'.

You can use this activity either to discuss together issues about safety or to reinforce what children might already know. The safety issues will depend on where you are living: for example, whether you are living in a refuge, on a busy road, in a block of flats, or a house. Some safety issues could be:

- Not opening the door without Mum or another adult present.

- Not giving out your address and telephone number without first asking Mum.

About safety

TAZ the tortoise is an expert at being safe. On the outside **TAZ** has a tough shell. He can just pull his head inside and be safe.

What are some of the rules that keep you safe in the place where you live? Can you write these messages down on **TAZ's** shell?

SECTION 2

TALKING ABOUT THINGS THAT MATTER

Activity 9: Wise ideas from Ollie

This activity is designed to place any talk or thoughts about upsetting times alongside good memories, so that you and your child can talk about any difficult memories from a base of a good time you have shared together. It may be important to spend a lot of time on this treasure chest because if one or both of you are feeling low it can be hard to think of any good times. Right now you may even be in the process of creating some 'good times'. These can be used for the treasure chest.

Sometimes in building a memory store for the treasure chest it is easier to think of milestones such as 'when you took your first steps'. While your child may not remember this moment, it may have been shared and exciting at the time. Other times might just be very small but important – a time they made you laugh, a shared joke, tucking them into bed at night, a take-away in front of the TV, a time you played together. Try and explore with your child a time they remember which was important for them. It may have involved other people. You may like to stay with just this first part of the activity until you have a number of 'good times' in the treasure chest. Remember that small incidents, not big events, usually make up the treasure chest.

The second part of the activity asks you and your child to talk about/draw any memories that upset them. Many young children are very 'present-centred' and may genuinely not have any sense of past upsetting memories which they want to put in the balloon. Other children may not be able to find the words to say what these memories are. Perhaps you could give them crayons and say: 'If you were feeling hurt or angry about something, what colour would you want and would you like to draw something in the balloon?' Some children will be very clear and have something they want to put in the balloon. It may have nothing to do with domestic abuse. The important message for your child is that the door is open for them to talk with you about things which upset them.

Sometimes you may find it distressing to find out about things which have upset your child. It is important that you listen to your child's experience openly. You may like to say you are concerned that this happened to them and ask them about what might help at the moment ('I'm really sorry that you had to live with this feeling/or that you saw this and were upset'). You may like to reinforce how positive it is that your child feels able to talk to you about these important things. It says very good things about your relationship if they are able to talk with you about these things ('I'm really pleased you are able to talk with me about this'). However, remember that it is not your child's role to support you if you are upset – find someone to talk to. Talk to a worker or with a trusted friend or family member, or ring a helpline. Remember also not to make promises you can't keep. If you are thinking about returning to the relationship, don't promise that this will never happen again.

Please finish this activity by going back to the treasure chest, so that you are always bringing out and building up a story of positive things in your relationship.

Wise ideas from OLLIE: talking about things that matter

OLLIE has been having a quiet time lately, sitting on her perch thinking 'wise thoughts'. She has an idea for you and your mum.

My Special Memories

STOP

GETTING WORRIED

KEEP GOING

OLLIE's idea for you and Mum
Think about something special that has happened. It might be now or in the past, a big thing or a little thing – just one thing that meant a lot to you and one thing that meant a lot to Mum. Put your special memories in the treasure chest and talk about them together.

Memories which upset me

In the balloon write down or draw something that made you feel scared, angry or hurt. You and Mum may like to spend some time telling each other about this. Then finish off with another special memory for the treasure chest.

Activity 10: More about us

This activity is another 'getting to know you' exercise. While you might know a lot about your child, they may know very little about you. It is an activity that leaves space for talking about enjoyable parts of your lives (however small or long ago) as well as leaving the door open to talk about more serious issues.

Again, it is an activity which helps your child to develop their sense of self and self-esteem. Helping them to say something about 'who they are' in relation to you is also an important part of building their relationship with you.

More about us

CAS the caterpillar and **JAS** the butterfly want to know more about you. Finish the sentence – first you and then Mum.

I like it when . . . .

. . . .

Mum likes it when . . . .

. . . .

I am unhappy when . . . .

. . . .

Mum is unhappy when . . . .

. . . .

I laugh when . . . .

. . . .

Mum laughs when . . . .

. . . .

Something I'd like to try is . . . .

. . . .

Something Mum would like to try is . . . .

. . . .

I have fun when . . . .

. . . .

STOP

GETTING
WORRIED

KEEP GOING

Mum enjoys herself when . . . .

. . . .

When I am alone I . . . .

When Mum is alone she . . . .

. . . .

When I am with friends I like to . . . .

. . . .

When Mum is with friends she likes to . . . .

. . . .

I get angry when . . . .

. . . .

Mum gets angry when . . . .

. . . .

Something I feel good about is . . . .

. . . .

Something Mum feels good about is . . . .

. . . .

Other things I would like to add . . . .

. . . .

. . . .

. . . .

Other things Mum would like to add . . . .

. . . .

. . . .

. . . .

STOP

GETTING WORRIED

KEEP GOING

Activity 11: A story about Nibbles and Prickles

No book for children is complete without a story. Stories and reading with children can be an important way of finding 'quality time' together. It can also make a very important contribution to your child's education. Children who have been read to or who enjoy reading can show very different levels of achievement later in life regardless of difficult life experiences.

This story is written so that your child can be actively involved. You will need to point to each word so that your child can follow where you are up to and say 'Nibbles' when they see the picture of the squirrel, 'Prickles' when they see the picture of the hedgehog, and 'Grumbles' when they see the picture of the dog. If the story is too long for your child, then you may like to take it over two sessions, or finish off the story without your child's help on the second page. It may take some time for both of you to get the hang of reading the story together. Try it again! Children often enjoy being involved even if they find reading difficult or have not learnt to read yet.

There is obviously a 'message' in the story – keeping the door open for your child to talk to you or other people about things which are happening in their life.

A story about NIBBLES and PRICKLES

You will need to help Mum every time she comes to an animal picture. You tell Mum whether it is NIBBLES the squirrel or  **PRICKLES the hedgehog, or GRUMBLES the dog.**

the squirrel and the hedgehog are friends who

live in the woods close to a farm. As long as they

stay in the woods they have a happy life.

thinks that lives a dull life pottering around under

bushes digging up worms. comes to talk with at the

end of the day about his adventures deep in the woods.

likes to hear his stories but worries that is far too

adventurous for his own good.

It is autumn time and is collecting nuts and burying them

ready for the winter. knows there is a tree full of acorns near

the farmhouse. He wants to go there, but

there is a big, cross dog called **GRUMBLES** living in the yard.

is really worried about but is one of those

squirrels who 'wants to do things his own way'. (Does that

remind you of anyone you know?)

Early one morning dashes off to the farmyard. Through

the paddock, across the ditch, under the fence and into the yard

with the big tree. All is quiet. sees some acorns on the

ground – squirrel heaven!!

STOP

GETTING WORRIED

KEEP GOING

is so excited he doesn't see the dog running across the yard … Suddenly he hears barking … oh no!! is between him and the tree. is terrified and drops his acorns … is getting closer and closer … is terrified … throws himself under the fence … barks angrily.

curls up in a ditch trying not to hear the barking. stays there all day. At nightfall he makes his way back to the woods. Every noise makes him jump. crawls up the tree hoping that won't hear him. Although is very tired he can't sleep. He keeps remembering barking. is worried about her friend – where is he? did hear a rustle near tree. She keeps listening out for

If wanted to feel better what might she say or do that would help? What about:

NOTHING IS SO BAD OR SCARY
THAT YOU CAN'T TALK ABOUT IT IF YOU WANT TO!

Do you think that might like a hug – even from a hedgehog??

The next day is **very** happy to see his good friend and to hang out with her.

They have **lots** to talk about.

STOP

GETTING WORRIED

KEEP GOING

Activity 12: Good things and bad things

In any place there are some things which are fun and enjoyable and things which are dangerous or risky. This activity introduces this theme in a 'child friendly' way. You may like to help your child with the colouring in so that it is a shared activity. Don't worry about staying 'inside the lines'. Just add some colour!

Some children will enjoy colouring in with you, but others may need something more active. If you have access to a garden or backyard you could do the same activity by going outside and looking at things which are good and bad for butterflies and caterpillars (and/or children). Don't forget to take a ball or something else for playing outdoors, or even a jar for collecting things.

Good things and bad things

Hey, **JAS** the butterfly and **CAS** the caterpillar are back playing in their garden. As in any place there are good things and bad things, scary things and interesting things.

Can you draw lines from **CAS** to one good thing and one bad thing for caterpillars? Can you draw lines from **JAS** to one good thing and one bad thing for butterflies? Mum may need to help you.

You might also like to colour in some of the picture.

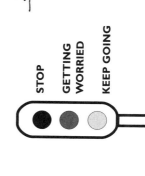

STOP

GETTING WORRIED

KEEP GOING

Activity 13: Good times and bad times

This activity has similar themes to the treasure chest and balloon. It provides another way of talking about good memories and things which may still be worrying your child. You may feel that having covered this once you can move on to the next activity and skip this one. However, drawing the house may reconnect with a different set of important experiences. Again, the worrying things they want to talk about may have nothing to do with domestic abuse. Remember just to be open to whatever your child has to say. There are no right or wrong answers.

This is a two-part activity. If you do the first part about a time when your child feels angry or hurt or sad, then find time to remember a happy time or a better time. Make sure that you can also put a happy memory into the house – particularly if it is one connected to your child. Children enjoy being reminded of stories about themselves which are positive. It is a very important part of building their confidence in themselves. Again, these can be very small incidents. Sometimes these are the most precious.

Good times and bad times in the place you used to live

Just like **CAS** and **JAS**, you have had good times and bad times, fun times and times when you might have been scared. **JAS** and **CAS** have come to visit your house (don't worry about tidying up your room, they live in a garden where there are lots of weeds – they like it that way). Can you draw or tell them about one time when you felt angry or hurt or scared about something that happened. On the next page remember one good time when you felt happy or had a lot of fun. Mum might also like to add her own memory of a good time to yours.

A hurt, angry or scary time

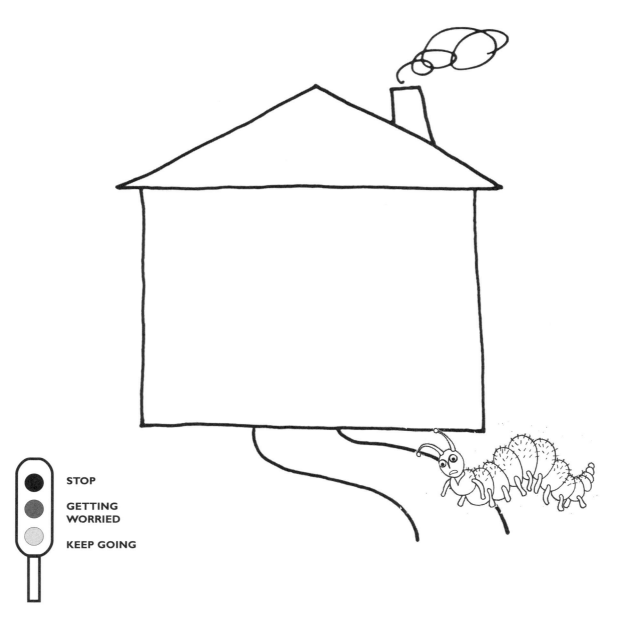

STOP

GETTING
WORRIED

KEEP GOING

A happy or fun time

STOP

GETTING
WORRIED

KEEP GOING

Activity 14: BAS talks about changes in families

Take your time with this activity. You may be able to do this very quickly or it might be an activity that you come back to at different times. The second page takes you through one way of doing this activity, but there are lots of other ways.

Sometimes children have very complicated family trees with different sets of grandparents, uncles and aunts. They might have stepfamilies or people who have acted as uncles, aunts or father figures. In families where the extended family is or has been very important you may need to put many more apples on the tree, or ask someone to photocopy the family tree so that you can have one tree for your side of the family and another tree for their father/father-figure side of the family.

Sometimes you or your child may have unhappy memories about some of these people, or there may be losses due to death or divorce. Sometimes you will have photos that may help with this activity. Sometimes you may have had to leave these behind if you moved in a hurry.

It is an important part of building your child's identity to know who they are in relation to other family members, even if they are people they are not in contact with, or can't have contact with due to safety issues or because they are no longer alive. It can be very important to put these people into the child's family tree.

If your child can remember a story (or you can remember a story) about a family member, then this can be a way of making the family tree activity more interesting and can also tell you a lot more about people who are important to your child.

BAS talks about changes in families

BAS is the expert on changes. He's been everywhere and lived in different places and with different families. By going into a refuge or moving house, there might be changes in your family life. Who is in your family? With help from your mum you can write in the names of the members of your family on this family tree. You can add some more apples if there aren't enough.

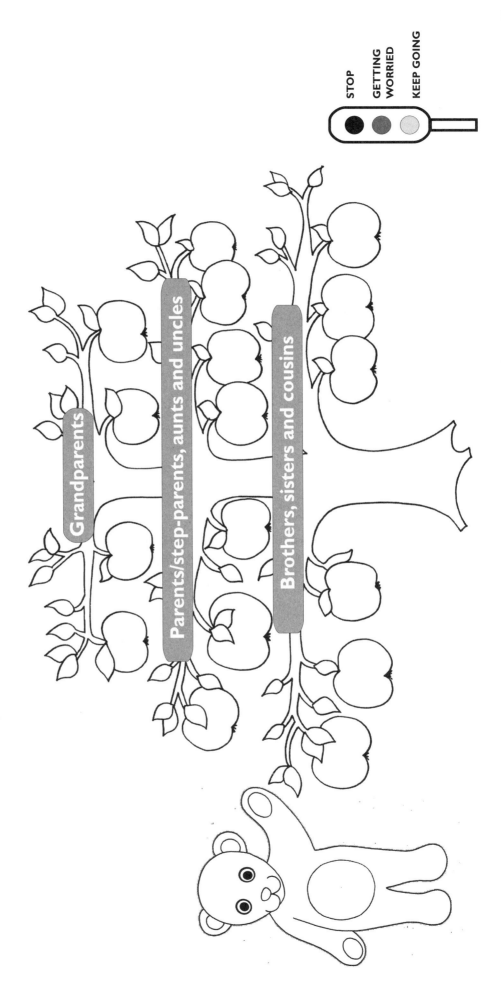

STOP

GETTING WORRIED

KEEP GOING

Sometimes people live with all their family members and other times not. Who do you live with now?

. . . .

. . . .

. . . .

Take one family member and talk about a memory you have about that person.

. . . .

. . . .

. . . .

. . . .

. . . .

Can you and Mum talk about the changes in your family?

If there are lots of changes, you might like to just take one name on the tree and talk about what that change means to you. (You could come back to this sheet and talk about other people another time.)

. . . .

. . . .

. . . .

. . . .

STOP

GETTING WORRIED

. . . .

. . . .

KEEP GOING

. . . .

. . . .

Activity 15: Talking about my dad

This activity is written for children who are no longer living with their fathers. Skip this activity if this is not the situation for you and your child.

For some mothers and children this can be a very tough issue to explore. For other children and their mothers it is easy. It may be more complicated if there is a father-figure who is not the child's birth father but who is, or has been, in their lives. You will need to be clear who your child is talking about when they do this activity. Leave it to them to choose.

When there has been domestic abuse and if the child's father is the abuser, then the issue of how a child feels about their father can sometimes be confusing. There may equally be important issues to explore if the child's father was not involved in domestic abuse but does not have regular contact with the child. Children may have very clear feelings or feel very confused.

This is an area which can be particularly difficult for you as a mother. There are no right answers. You may need a lot of support from a worker to deal with the feelings your child raises. There may be some very practical issues which need to be discussed. Children may feel that they like the contact/lack of contact they have with their fathers, or they may feel very unhappy about current arrangements.

Whatever is happening you should try to make safety (both emotional and physical) a priority, though sometimes due to court decisions this may not be in your control.

You may not be able to solve any problems that have been raised. Remember also that if you come back to this activity at a later date, it might show something different to both of you. If you can talk openly about what is often a very difficult subject, then you have both done brilliantly. Give yourselves a treat!!

Talking about my dad

OLLIE is a wise owl and knows that not all children feel the same. Children can have lots of different feelings at the same time, and feelings can change every day.

If you no longer live with your dad, you may have lots of different feelings about this. You might not know who your dad is, you might not have seen him for a long time, or you might see him lots of times.

Draw a picture of yourself in the circle. Draw lines to the feelings which you have when you think about your dad.

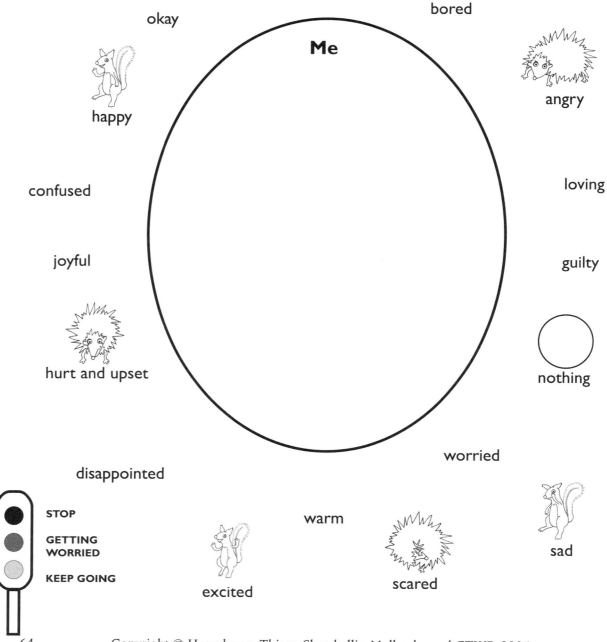

Copyright © Humphreys, Thiara, Skamballis, Mullender and CTWR 2006

Mum's thoughts

Talk with Mum about what you have drawn.

Other people

Are there any other people you need to talk to about your drawing?

. . . .

. . . .

You and Mum are ☆ stars ☆

Lots of kids and their mothers are not able to talk about these things.

Activity 16: TAZ imagines a happy time

Some children find it very difficult to go to bed at night. If you have never done an activity like this with your child, it could feel very strange at first – you may just end up laughing. It is clearly quite difficult to do if you have more than one child and they go to bed at different times. However, helping your child to find a 'happy picture' which they can come back to is a real gift. They may like to make up their own picture, or you may like to help them make up a picture which 'fits for them', or just sitting with them for a little while they go to sleep may be enough.

Also having a 'wind down time' when children learn to breathe a little more slowly and in a relaxed way is great for them to learn at an early age.

Again, having a quiet time at the end of the day to share together can be important 'quality time' for both of you if it is at all possible.

Drawing or sticking things onto the Magic Place sheet the next day can help keep the picture 'alive' and accessible to your child.

TAZ imagines a happy time

This is a good activity for going to bed. Mum can read this to you to help you go to sleep.

Sometimes this is easier if you **close your eyes**.

TAZ the tortoise is in the woods and wants to sleep. But his friend **JAS** the butterfly won't stop talking (she can talk the petals off a daisy). **TAZ** wants to take **JAS** to a magic place where she feels safe and happy.

Mum can read very slowly. You and Mum can go to this magic place together.

Once upon a time, there was a child, a mother and a beautiful butterfly … The butterfly wanted to go to a sunny place … Mum wanted to go to a place which was pretty and relaxing … The child wanted to go to a place which was fun and happy …

Take a deep breath and then breathe out slowly … you have arrived in a garden by the sea … the sun is shining … the butterfly finds a lovely flower to sit on … Mum and you walk together across the green grass to look at the sea … a big sandy hill leads down to the beach beside the sea … Mum finds a place on the warm sand and sits down …

You both take a big breath and breathe out slowly … the child takes a big jump … leaping and rolling in the sand … the child looks up … Mum is laughing and waving … the afternoon is spent running and playing in the sand and the sea … at last you both lie on the warm sand …

Breathe deeply … relax … the butterfly sits quietly on a nearby flower … everything is still … except the sound of your breathing.

STOP

GETTING WORRIED

KEEP GOING

Your magic place

You might like to draw the picture you made in your mind – or you could make a picture by sticking things on a sheet of paper that remind you of your magic place.

STOP

GETTING
WORRIED

KEEP GOING

Activity 17: Feelings tree

This is a good activity for helping both of you look together at the different changes you have made. Some mothers and children use the 'feelings tree' as a 'check-in' to point to how they are feeling today, without having to really say anything or explain themselves.

The 'feelings tree' can be used with any age group. It is a way of being able to share with each other how you are feeling now and sometimes see where you may have come from.

You can sometimes ask further questions such as: 'What has happened that makes you feel like this today?' 'Is there anything I can do to help you to another part of the tree?'

Feelings tree

Life has its ups and downs. Can you and Mum talk about where you both are on the tree at the moment? You may have been in more than one place on the tree over the past few months. Can you tell each other about this?

SECTION 3

MOVING ON

Activity 18: Keeping track of my life

This activity does just what it says – keeping track of your life. Particularly if children have made a number of moves it can be very confusing for them to make sense of where they have come from. Trying to fit the jigsaw pieces in their lives together so that they can hold onto an overall picture can be important – for you as well as them.

Children who worked on developing this activity seemed to be particularly interested in their mother's story, of what they were doing or where they were at the same age. Putting two stories (yours and your child's) together can be a very important way of building your relationship.

Keeping track of my life

Sometimes things seem to change fast. One minute you're living in one place, next minute somewhere else. **CAS** and **JAS** know more about these things than most. One minute **CAS** was a caterpillar, next minute a butterfly – that's a pretty big change for one life!! What about you? Would you recognise yourself as a baby? With Mum's help why don't you start to keep track of your life, year by year. You might like to put in:

● where you were living

● who was living in your home at different times (don't forget relatives, friends or pets)

● when brothers and sisters were born

● going to nursery or starting school.

You might like to ask Mum where she was at the same age and where she went to school.

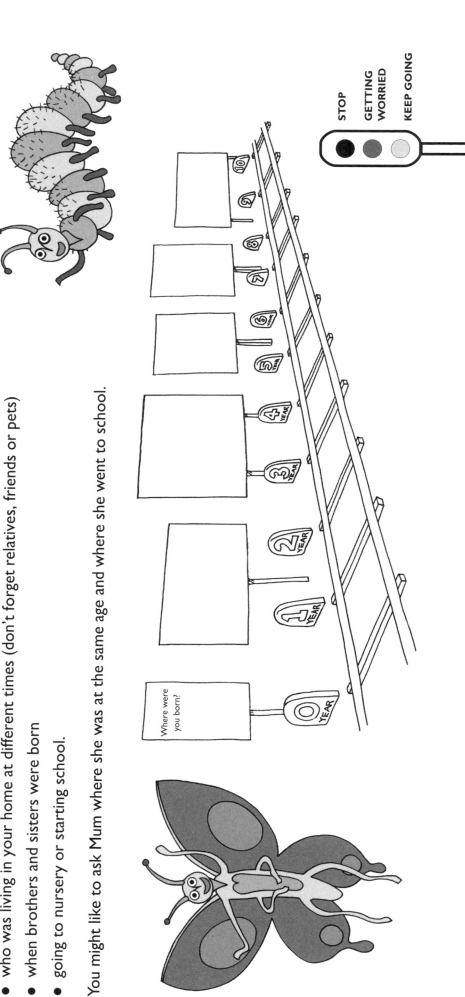

STOP

GETTING WORRIED

KEEP GOING

Activity 19: Moving on

This activity is designed for children who are about to move house – maybe from the refuge. Children may be very anxious or very excited about moving from one place to another. It can be very helpful to talk about where you are going. They may have a lot of questions, or not know what to ask about. This activity is just a beginning. It helps children to prepare for change if some of their questions have been answered, or if you understand the things which are important to them.

Once you have moved, you may like to go back to the 'Keeping track of my life' activity and write in the change.

Moving on

BAS is the expert for moves and changes. Sometimes he leaves one house and moves to another without warning. Sometimes he has moved back to his old house. He knows that the same things can happen to children.

You might have some questions for Mum about where you are going next if you are going to move. If she doesn't have the answers yet, you can tell her what is important to you so she will know.

We have put in some questions but you might have lots more.

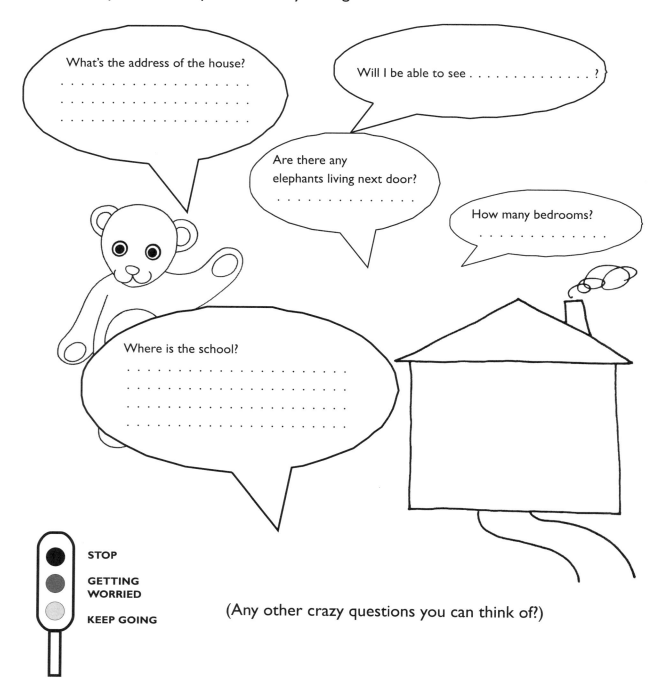

What's the address of the house?

Will I be able to see . . . . ?

Are there any elephants living next door?

How many bedrooms?

Where is the school?

STOP

GETTING WORRIED

KEEP GOING

(Any other crazy questions you can think of?)

Activity 20: Safe hands

This is a well-known activity which is often used with children in schools. It helps children think about adults who they can contact and also helps you to support your child in expanding their network of people they can talk to. It gives your child the message that asking for help or talking to people when they are worried about things is okay. Children often want to put in pets, imaginary friends and soft toys.

If you have had to live with lots of secrets and keep important aspects of your life hidden, encouraging your child to talk with people other than yourself may not feel comfortable. This is a very understandable, dare we say 'normal', reaction. Again, this is an area where you may need some support from other people.

Safe hands

TAZ and **PRICKLES** have been having a talk in the garden.

PRICKLES: Hey **TAZ**, I've got this friend **NIBBLES** that I'm worried about. She's been in some hairy situations lately (that's saying something when you've only got spines!!). She's talked to me, which is great, but I feel like I should give her some advice about safety. You're good on that sort of stuff.

TAZ: Hmmmmmm … (sorry, he's asleep)

… I think that means it's over to you, Mum.

Could I suggest that you ask . . . . to do the following things:

(name)

- Take a pencil and draw around his/her hand.

- On each finger put an adult's name who can be trusted and who he/she could call if they need help (it might be someone you know like an aunty, or it might be a teacher or a policeman/woman).

- On the palm of the hand, put the name of someone else or something that . . . . likes to talk to (a favourite toy, a friend).

(name)
- For children in the UK, on one of the fingers put the number of Childline: 0800 1111.

TAZ (who seems to be awake at last): I think you should tell **NIBBLES** that **there is nothing so awful or so small that she can't tell someone about it**. There are lots of friends around who will help.

PRICKLES: I'll tell **NIBBLES**. It sounds like good advice for everyone.

STOP

GETTING WORRIED

KEEP GOING

Safe hands

STOP

GETTING
WORRIED

KEEP GOING

Activity 21: My space

Sometimes children need a space which is just for them to draw or write whatever they want.

Some children might like to write a letter (not for sending) to someone who has upset or hurt them, or made them angry. They could start with DEAR...

Other children may just like to have a space for drawing whatever they like. They might like to use it for when they are feeling unhappy, or they might like to use it to draw something which makes them feel good.

My space

Activity 22: Looking backwards and looking forwards

This activity is designed for mothers and children who are leaving the place where they are living at the moment. This may be a refuge, a hostel or the home of friends or relatives.

It is easier to move on if you are able to say goodbye and thank people who have been important. Helping your child to take these steps gives them time to prepare for a move and to appreciate that they may have made relationships with people who are important.

Taking the time to make a card will also allow other people to say positive things to your child – an important part of building their self-esteem.

Some children may prefer to make up a text message or write a message on the flowers. Let your child choose the activity they prefer. They may want to do both.

It is a three-step activity which you need to follow through on the three separate sheets.

1. Your child writes a message in the flower or the phone about what they will miss.

2. You write a message in the flower on p.85. This allows your child to know your feelings too.

3. On the flower on p.86 your child writes a message that they want to give to someone who has been special to them. Cut out the flower so that your child can give the card to the person who has been important to them.

Looking backwards, looking forwards

OLLIE is flying around. She is all a-flutter as people seem to be leaving. She is worried that they haven't had time to say goodbye properly to people who have been important to them. She knows that it is easier to move on if you say goodbye to people who have been special to you.

Things or people I will miss

Choose either the flower or the phone on the next page (or both!). In the middle of the flower, write 'I will miss'. On the petals, write or draw the things or people you will miss.

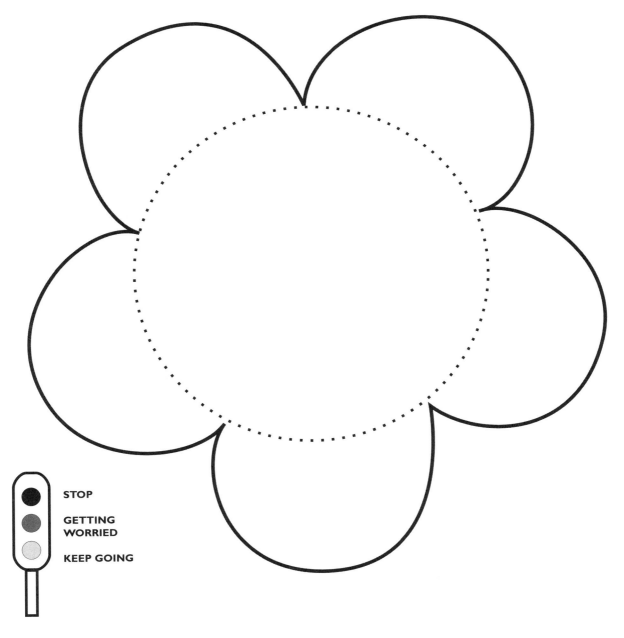

STOP

GETTING WORRIED

KEEP GOING

83

In the window of the phone, write 'I will miss', and then write or draw the things or people you will miss.

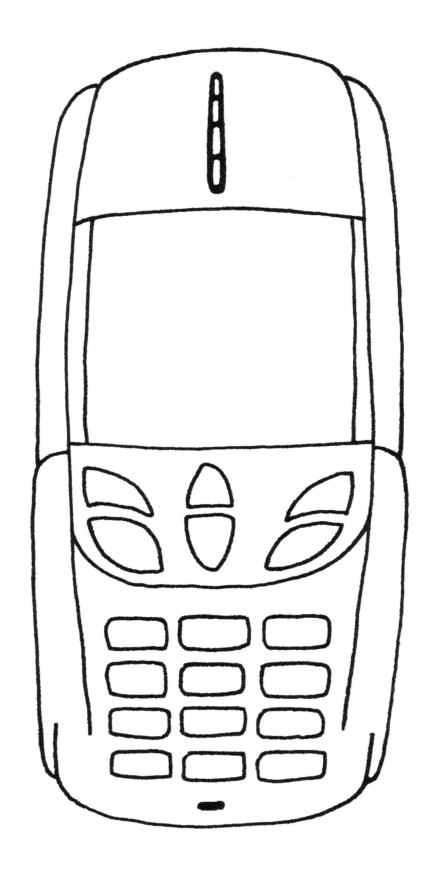

Things or people that Mum will miss

In the middle write 'I will miss'. On the petals, write or draw the things you will miss.

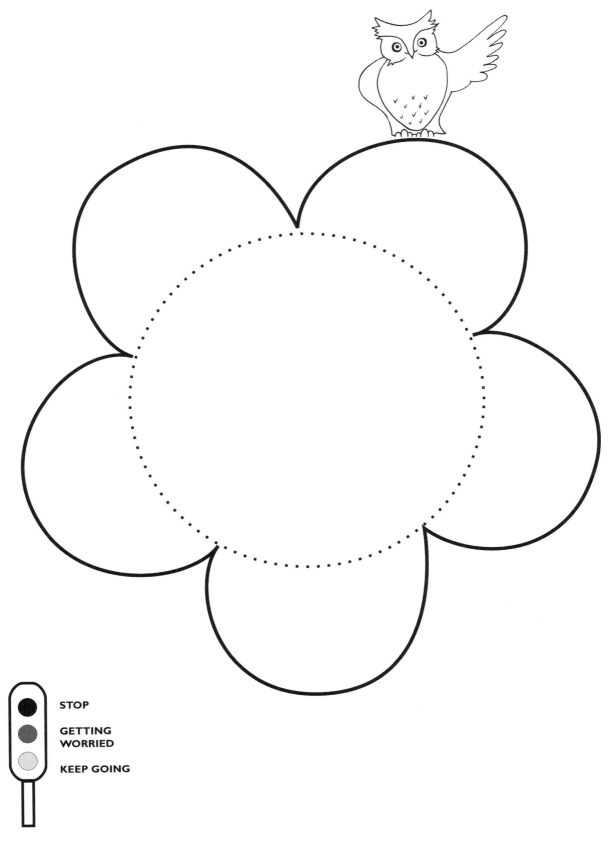

STOP

GETTING
WORRIED

KEEP GOING

Flower messages

This flower is for you to leave a message to someone really special to you.

- With Mum's help, cut out the flower.

- In the centre you could write a message for someone who has been important to you: for example, 'I will miss you' or 'Thanks for your help'. Make up your own message.

- Fold the petals over (you may like to colour them in first) and give the flower message to your special person.

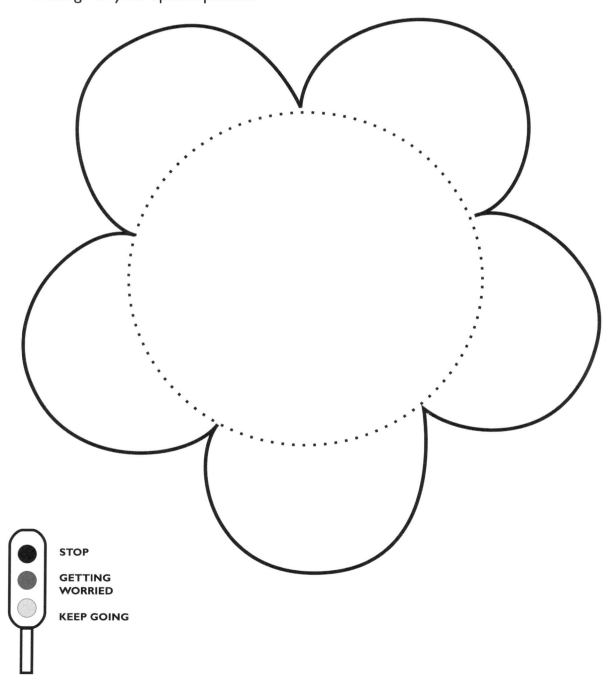

STOP

GETTING WORRIED

KEEP GOING

Last of all – your woodland friends TAZ, JAS, CAS, BAS, NIBBLES, PRICKLES and **OLLIE** say:

WELL DONE!

YOU AND YOUR MUM ARE BRILLIANT!

Certificate

Congratulations to:

....

for completing the activities in
Talking to My Mum

....
(Signature)

....
(Date)

Please fill in and give to the worker

Which activity do you want to comment on? . . . .

Date: . . . . Name: . . . .

Child's comments

What I felt about doing this activity sheet. Circle the face: ☺ 😐 ☹

Is this a good activity for other children?

Any comments?

. . . .

. . . .

. . . .

Mum's comments

How did it feel to work on this sheet with your child for both your child and you? For example:

Was it upsetting? . . . .

If yes, why? . . . .

Child couldn't concentrate? Why? . . . .

Was it a really good way to spend time together? . . . .

Was the activity suitable for your child's age? If not, was it too hard or too easy?

. . . .

There may be all sorts of other things you want to say below.

. . . .

. . . .

Thank you for your time.

Conclusion

This workbook is only one of a thousand ways for mothers and children to spend time together.

We are also hoping that people who are more 'techie' than us will develop new interactive ideas for websites and computers. When developing the activities in this workbook with workers, mothers and children, we found there is sometimes a 'technical divide' between mothers and their children. We also found that many of the refuges we were working with at the beginning didn't have computers that were readily available for mothers and children. Therefore we have started with basic everyday activities which most mothers and children can do together needing nothing more than pencil and paper. However, the electronic media with CD-ROMs, interactive websites and videos would suit the needs of many women and young people and we assume these will be developed in the future.

We are also aware that some children are very active and need to be engaged in more physical activities than are provided in this workbook. Here are some suggestions, and we know that you will be able to think of many more.

- If there is a playground close by or a backyard, then go out and play. Older children could be encouraged to kick a ball, throw a frisbee or go for a walk.

- Put on some music. Listen together, make up a dance or do karaoke. See how many words of the song you know.

- Go on an outing together.

- Try outdoor activities you know your child likes – swimming, running, climbing, football, netball, cycling, kite flying, etc.

- If you live in a refuge, ask the workers whether you can go to the playroom and play with dough or clay. All sorts of feelings can be expressed with dough and clay – have a go together.

- Painting activities can allow mothers and children to have a go at 'free painting', looking for colours to express the way they feel at the moment. Or they may like to paint things they miss and things which make them happy or feel at peace.

- Children often love playing with puppets. If these are in the playroom, then mothers and children may like to strike up a conversation between two puppets. Mum's puppet could ask or talk about all sorts of things, such as: favourite places the child's puppet would like to visit; three puppet wishes; building a fantasy home together for the puppets; going on an adventure together; what upsets puppets; making puppets safe; building a cubbyhouse for the puppets where they can feel safe.

- If you have a camera (some disposable cameras are quite cheap), then taking photos can be a great activity for older children.

Perhaps make your own list of things here which you have done or might like to do together.

Useful contacts

UK

National Domestic Violence Helpline
Tel: 0808 2000 247

This is a freephone 24-hour domestic violence helpline.

Women's Aid
Website: www.womensaid.org.uk

This website provides comprehensive information for all survivors of domestic abuse in the UK.

Children

Childline
Tel: 0800 1111
Website: www.childline.org.uk

ChildLine is a free helpline for children and young people in the UK. Children and young people can call to talk about any problem (including domestic abuse). Counsellors are there to help sort out problems.

The Hideout
Website: www.thehideout.org.uk

Special website developed by Women's Aid for children living with domestic abuse.

NSPCC
Tel: 0808 800 5000
Website: www.nspcc.org.uk/kidszone

Website for children and young people with helpful information and support across a wide range of areas.

Black and minority ethnic women and children

Apna Ghar
Tel: 0207 474 1547 (24 hours)

Apna Ghar is a helpline for Asian women experiencing domestic violence. Languages spoken include: Bengali, Hindi, Punjabi, Gujerati, Tamil and Urdu.

Muslim Women's Helpline
Tel: 0208 904 8193; 0208 908 6715 (Monday to Friday, 10 am – 4 pm).
Email: mwhl@amrnet.demon.co.uk
Website: www.mwhl.org

Muslim Women's Helpline provides a telephone counselling service for all Muslim women, regardless of ethnicity. It provides information and refers to local services when appropriate.

Newham Asian Women's Project
Tel: 020 8472 0528
Email: info@nawp.org
Website: www.nawp.org

Newham Asian Women's Project is based in the London Borough of Newham. The project supports South Asian women who are experiencing domestic violence and offers a resource centre, refuges for women and children, counselling services and projects for teenagers and young women.

Southall Black Sisters
Tel: 020 8571 9595
Email: sbs@leonet.co.uk
Website: www.southallblacksisters.org.uk

Southall Black Sisters is a resource centre mainly for Asian, African and Afro-Caribbean women. It provides advice and information on domestic violence, racial harassment and welfare, immigration and matrimonial rights.

Disabled women

UK Disability Forum
Website: www.edfwomen.org.uk/abuse.htm

For disabled women experiencing domestic violence, the website gives information about getting help to tackle violence and abuse.

USA

National Domestic Violence Hotline
1 800 799 SAFE (7233)
Website: www.ndvh.org

Hotline advocates are available for victims and anyone calling on their behalf to provide crisis intervention, safety planning, information and referrals to agencies in all 50 states, Puerto Rico and the US Virgin Islands. Assistance is available in English and Spanish with access to more than 140 languages through interpreter services.

National Coalition Against Domestic Violence
Website: www.ncadv.org

Provides good information about protecting yourself and making safety plans. There are 50 state coalitions and contact information is provided in the resources section of the website.

The Family Violence Prevention Fund
Website: www.endabuse.org/

The website contains information relevant to immigrant women and children.

Childhelp USA
1 800 4 A CHILD (1 800 422 4453)

This is the most widely known child abuse hotline in the US.

Australia

Services in Australia are based in different states and any of the general helpline numbers will provide information on more specialised services.

National helpline: 1800 200 526
Website: http://ofw.facs.gov.au/womens_safety_agenda/domestic_violence_help

ACT	6280 0900
New South Wales	1800 656 463
Northern Territory	1800 019 116
Queensland	1800 811 811
South Australia	1800 800 098
Tasmania	1800 633 937
Victoria (Melbourne)	9373 0123
Victoria (rural)	1800 015 188
Western Australia	1800 007 339

For children and young people the following contacts are available:

Kids Help Line
Tel: 1800 55 1800
Email: counsellor@kidshelp.com.au (for email counselling)
Website: www.kidshelp.com.au (web counselling: Monday to Friday, 3 pm – 9 pm)

Kids Help Line is a national counselling service for young people aged 5 to 18 years. It is a free, anonymous and confidential service which kids can call or they can chat to a counsellor online.

Canada

Services in Canada are based in different provinces and any of the general helpline numbers will provide information on more specialised services.

National Domestic Violence Hotline
1 800 363 9010

Domestic Violence Hotline (which also serves the US)
1 800 799 723324

Young people's bilingual helpline
1 800 363 9010

National Clearinghouse on Family Violence
Website: www.phac-aspc.gc.ca/ncfv-cnivf/familyviolence

Each state also has its own domestic violence resources for women and children and the National Clearinghouse on Family Violence provides resources and information for each state.